204052

7-22-09

D1649143

Time to Eat at the White House

VOID

By Marge Kennedy

Children's Press®
An Imprint of Scholastic Inc.
New York Toronto London Auckland Sydney
Mexico City New Delhi Hong Kong
Danbury, Connecticut

These content vocabulary word builders are for grades 1–2.

Subject Consultant: Eli J. Lesser, MA, Director of Education,
National Constitution Center, Philadelphia, Pennsylvania

Reading Consultant: Cecilia Minden-Cupp, PhD, Early Literacy Consultant and Author,
Chapel Hill, North Carolina

Photographs © 2009: AP Images: back cover, 5 bottom left, 18, 19 bottom (Charles Dharapak), cover, 4 bottom left, 5 top left, 6, 12, 17, 23 bottom right (Ron Edmonds), 23 top left (Evan Vucci), 9; Corbis Images/Yuri Gripas/Reuters: 1, 13; Getty Images: 5 top right, 8 (Quentin Bacon), 15 (Tim Graham), 5 bottom right, 14 (Aude Guerrucci), 2, 4 bottom right, 16 (Saul Loeb/AFP), 23 top right (Tim Sloan/AFP), 19 top (Chip Somodevilla), 11 (Diana Walker/Time Life Pictures), 23 bottom left (Alex Wong); iStockphoto: 20 (Jani Bryson), 21 bottom (Elena Elisseeva), 21 top right (Donald Erickson), 21 top left (Susan Trigg); Courtesy of the Jimmy Carter Library: 7; Photolibrary/ Burke Triolo/Brand X Pictures: 4 top, 10; www.whitehouse.gov: 21 hot chocolate recipe.

Series Design: Simonsays Design!
Art Direction, Production, and Digital Imaging: Scholastic Classroom Magazines

Library of Congress Cataloging-in-Publication Data

Kennedy, Marge M., 1950-
Time to Eat at the White House / Marge Kennedy.
    p. cm. — (Scholastic news nonfiction readers)
Includes bibliographical references and index.
ISBN 13: 978-0-531-21098-7 (lib. bdg.)   978-0-531-22436-6 (pbk.)
ISBN 10: 0-531-21098-7 (lib. bdg.)   0-531-22436-8 (pbk.)
1. Dinners and dining—Washington (D.C.)—Juvenile literature. 2. Cooks—Washington (D.C.)—Juvenile literature. 3. White House (Washington, D.C.)—Juvenile literature. I. Title. II. Series.
TX737.K3878 2009
641.509753—dc22   2008039656

CONTENTS

WORD HUNT

Look for these words as you read. They will be in **bold**.

broccoli
(**brok**-uh-lee)

kitchen
(**kich**-uhn)

menu
(**men**-yoo)

4

chef
(shef)

chowder
(**chow**-dur)

pastry
(**pay**-stree)

state dinner
(state **din**-ur)

What's Cooking at the White House?

Do you know what the President eats for dinner?

Anything he wants!

A **chef** cooks the foods the President likes best.

chef

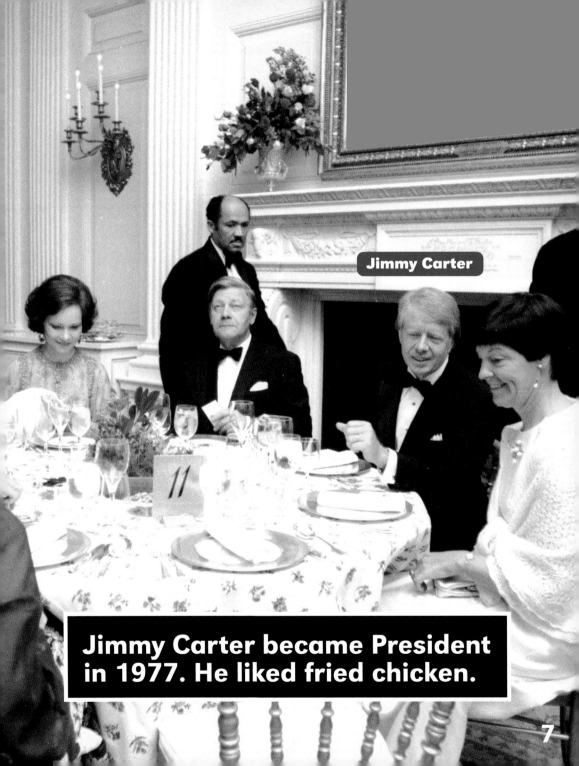

Jimmy Carter

Jimmy Carter became President in 1977. He liked fried chicken.

President Kennedy liked to eat fish **chowder**. Sometimes he asked for it two or three days in a row!

Chowder is a kind of soup. It is made with milk and vegetables.

chowder

John F. Kennedy became President in 1961. Here he is with his son, John.

President George H. W. Bush did not like **broccoli**. The chef served spinach instead. The President liked spinach better.

broccoli

George H.W. Bush became President in 1989. He often ate lunch in his office.

There is more than one chef at the White House. There is more than one **kitchen** too. There are five of each!

Why are there so many chefs and kitchens?

kitchen

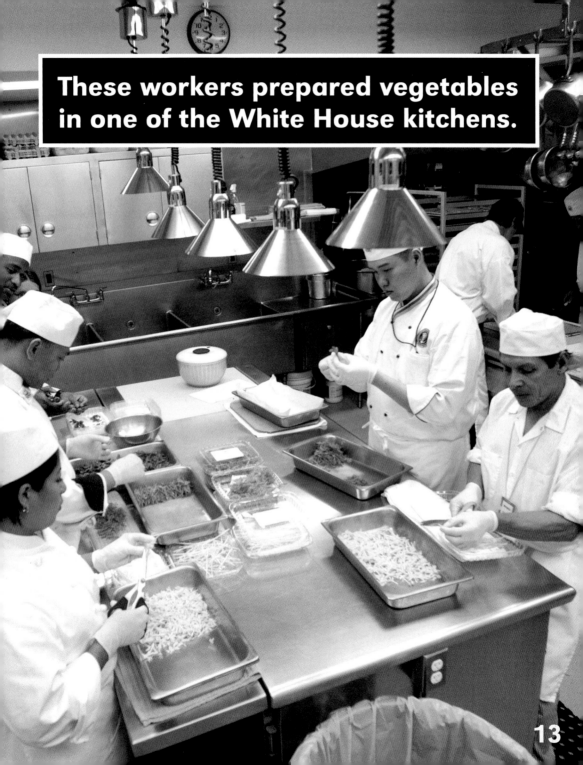

These workers prepared vegetables in one of the White House kitchens.

There are many chefs
and kitchens because the
President has many guests.

More than 100 people may
come to a **state dinner**.
A state dinner is a dinner
party with important guests.

**state
dinner**

The Queen of England came to this state dinner in 2007.

Queen Elizabeth II

It takes a lot of work to get ready for a state dinner. The head chef plans the **menu**, or what foods to serve.

All the chefs help cook the food.

menu

There is a lot of cooking to do for a big party! Everyone works together.

One chef makes only desserts! This is the **pastry** chef. Pastry is a kind of dessert.

If you lived in the White House, what would you ask the chefs to make for *you*?

pastry

The pastry chef and his helpers made all these desserts. Yum!

A WHITE HOUSE RECIPE

President George W. Bush's wife, Laura, liked to make tasty hot chocolate for friends at the White House. You can make this same White House treat at home! Make sure an adult helps.

Mrs. Bush's Hot Chocolate

INGREDIENTS:

6 tablespoons unsweetened cocoa
6 tablespoons sugar
pinch of salt
2 ½ cups milk
2 ½ cups light cream
½ teaspoon vanilla
pinch of cinnamon
whipped cream

DIRECTIONS:

1. Mix cocoa, sugar, and salt in a saucepan.
2. Add milk. Heat to dissolve.
3. Add light cream, vanilla, and cinnamon. Heat to just under boiling.
4. Mix very well and pour into warm mugs.
5. Top with whipped cream.

Makes about 5 cups.

YOUR NEW WORDS

broccoli (**brok**-uh-lee) a green vegetable that looks like a tree

chef (shef) someone whose job is to cook for other people

chowder (**chow**-dur) a thick soup made with milk and vegetables

kitchen (**kich**-uhn) a room where food is cooked or prepared

menu (**men**-yoo) a list of foods being served at a special meal or in a restaurant

pastry (**pay**-stree) desserts made with dough, such as pies and tarts

state dinner (state **din**-ur) a fancy dinner at the White House with the President and important guests

FOUR AMAZING WHITE HOUSE DESSERTS

Sugar Giraffe

Gingerbread House

Holiday Cookies

Chocolate Dog and Chocolate Egg

INDEX

FIND OUT MORE

Book:
Larkin, Tanya. *What Was Cooking in Dolley Madison's White House?*
New York: PowerKids Press, 2007.

Website:
The White House
www.whitehouse.gov/chef

MEET THE AUTHOR
Marge Kennedy is waiting for a dinner invitation to
the White House.